50 Legendary Crab and Lobster Recipes

By: Kelly Johnson

Table of Contents

- Lobster Newberg
- Crab Cakes
- Lobster Bisque
- Crab Rangoon
- Lobster Roll
- Crab Stuffed Mushrooms
- Lobster Tail with Garlic Butter
- Crab Legs with Old Bay Seasoning
- Lobster Mac and Cheese
- Crab and Corn Chowder
- Lobster Thermidor
- Crab Imperial
- Lobster and Shrimp Scampi
- Crab Dip
- Lobster En Papillote
- Crab Claws with Lemon Butter
- Lobster Tails with Herb Butter
- Crab Salad
- Lobster Poutine
- Crab Fritters
- Lobster Po' Boy Sandwich
- Crab Ceviche
- Lobster Ravioli
- Crab and Avocado Salad
- Lobster and Crab Stuffed Lobster
- Crab Louie Salad
- Lobster Pappardelle
- Crabmeat Omelette
- Lobster and Crab Linguine
- Crab Boil
- Lobster Tacos
- Crab and Spinach Stuffed Artichokes
- Lobster Bisque Gratin
- Crab Wellington
- Lobster with Mango Salsa

- Crab Mac and Cheese
- Lobster and Corn Fritters
- Crab Alfredo
- Lobster Salad with Lemon Vinaigrette
- Crab-Stuffed Bell Peppers
- Lobster Sautéed with Garlic and Wine
- Crab Croquettes
- Lobster Tail with Lemon Aioli
- Crab-Stuffed Mushrooms
- Lobster and Crab Risotto
- Crab and Lobster Bisque Soup
- Lobster and Crab Ramen
- Crab and Lobster Gratin
- Lobster and Crab Cakes with Remoulade
- Crab and Lobster Bruschetta

Lobster Newberg

Ingredients:

- 2 lobster tails, cooked and chopped
- 4 large eggs
- 1/2 cup heavy cream
- 1 tablespoon brandy or cognac
- 1/4 cup lobster stock
- 1 tablespoon butter
- 1/2 teaspoon paprika
- Salt and pepper to taste
- Fresh parsley for garnish

Instructions:

1. **Prepare the lobster:**
   Cook the lobster tails in boiling water for about 5-7 minutes, then chop the meat into bite-sized pieces.
2. **Make the custard:**
   In a saucepan, heat butter over medium heat. Whisk the eggs and heavy cream in a bowl. Add the brandy and lobster stock, and then pour this mixture into the pan. Stir constantly until the custard thickens (about 4-5 minutes).
3. **Combine the lobster:**
   Add the lobster meat to the custard, stirring gently. Season with salt, pepper, and paprika.
4. **Serve:**
   Spoon the lobster mixture into small serving dishes and garnish with fresh parsley.

Crab Cakes

Ingredients:

- 1 lb fresh crab meat, drained
- 1/2 cup breadcrumbs
- 1/4 cup mayonnaise
- 1 tablespoon Dijon mustard
- 1 egg, beaten
- 2 teaspoons Worcestershire sauce
- 1/2 teaspoon Old Bay seasoning
- 2 tablespoons fresh parsley, chopped
- Salt and pepper to taste
- Olive oil for frying

Instructions:

1. **Prepare the mixture:**
   In a bowl, combine crab meat, breadcrumbs, mayonnaise, Dijon mustard, egg, Worcestershire sauce, Old Bay seasoning, parsley, salt, and pepper. Mix gently to avoid breaking the crab meat too much.
2. **Form the cakes:**
   Shape the mixture into small patties (about 2-3 inches in diameter).
3. **Cook the crab cakes:**
   Heat olive oil in a skillet over medium heat. Fry the crab cakes for 3-4 minutes per side until golden and crispy.
4. **Serve:**
   Serve with tartar sauce or lemon wedges.

Lobster Bisque

Ingredients:

- 2 lobster tails, cooked and shells removed
- 1 tablespoon butter
- 1 onion, chopped
- 1 celery stalk, chopped
- 1 carrot, chopped
- 2 cloves garlic, minced
- 1/4 cup brandy or cognac
- 3 cups seafood stock
- 1 cup heavy cream
- 1 tablespoon tomato paste
- 1 teaspoon thyme
- Salt and pepper to taste

Instructions:

1. **Prepare the lobster stock:**
   In a large pot, heat butter over medium heat. Add the onion, celery, carrot, and garlic, cooking until softened (about 5 minutes). Add the lobster shells and cook for another 2 minutes. Pour in the brandy and let it simmer for 2 minutes.
2. **Make the bisque base:**
   Add the seafood stock, tomato paste, thyme, salt, and pepper. Bring to a boil, then reduce to a simmer for 20 minutes. Strain the stock to remove the solids.
3. **Finish the bisque:**
   Return the stock to the pot. Add the heavy cream and bring to a simmer. Chop the lobster meat and add it to the bisque. Cook for an additional 5 minutes until heated through.
4. **Serve:**
   Ladle the bisque into bowls and garnish with fresh parsley or a dollop of crème fraîche.

Crab Rangoon

Ingredients:

- 8 oz cream cheese, softened
- 1/2 cup crab meat, shredded
- 1/4 cup green onions, chopped
- 1 tablespoon soy sauce
- 1 teaspoon garlic powder
- 1/2 teaspoon Worcestershire sauce
- 10-12 wonton wrappers
- Vegetable oil for frying

Instructions:

1. **Prepare the filling:**
   In a bowl, combine cream cheese, crab meat, green onions, soy sauce, garlic powder, and Worcestershire sauce.
2. **Fill the wontons:**
   Place a teaspoon of the crab mixture in the center of each wonton wrapper. Wet the edges of the wrapper with water, then fold into a triangle and press the edges to seal.
3. **Fry the Rangoon:**
   Heat oil in a frying pan over medium-high heat. Fry the crab rangoon for 2-3 minutes until golden brown and crispy.
4. **Serve:**
   Drain on paper towels and serve with sweet and sour sauce.

Lobster Roll

Ingredients:

- 2 lobster tails, cooked and chopped
- 1/4 cup mayonnaise
- 1 tablespoon lemon juice
- 1 teaspoon Dijon mustard
- 2 hot dog buns (preferably buttered and toasted)
- Fresh parsley, chopped
- Salt and pepper to taste

Instructions:

1. **Prepare the lobster salad:**
   In a bowl, combine chopped lobster meat, mayonnaise, lemon juice, Dijon mustard, parsley, salt, and pepper. Mix gently.
2. **Assemble the roll:**
   Spoon the lobster mixture into the toasted buns.
3. **Serve:**
   Serve immediately with extra lemon wedges on the side.

Crab Stuffed Mushrooms

Ingredients:

- 12 large mushroom caps, stems removed
- 1/2 lb crab meat, shredded
- 1/4 cup cream cheese, softened
- 1/4 cup grated Parmesan cheese
- 1 tablespoon garlic, minced
- 1 tablespoon lemon juice
- 1 tablespoon fresh parsley, chopped
- Salt and pepper to taste
- Olive oil for drizzling

Instructions:

1. **Prepare the filling:**
   In a bowl, mix together crab meat, cream cheese, Parmesan cheese, garlic, lemon juice, parsley, salt, and pepper.
2. **Stuff the mushrooms:**
   Spoon the crab mixture into each mushroom cap.
3. **Bake:**
   Preheat the oven to 375°F (190°C). Place the stuffed mushrooms on a baking sheet and drizzle with olive oil. Bake for 15-20 minutes, until the mushrooms are tender and the stuffing is golden.
4. **Serve:**
   Serve warm as an appetizer.

Lobster Tail with Garlic Butter

Ingredients:

- 4 lobster tails, shells split
- 1/2 cup butter, melted
- 3 cloves garlic, minced
- 1 tablespoon lemon juice
- Fresh parsley, chopped
- Salt and pepper to taste

Instructions:

1. **Prepare the lobster tails:**
   Preheat the grill to medium-high heat. Using kitchen shears, split the lobster tails down the center. Gently pull the meat out of the shell, leaving it attached at the base.
2. **Make the garlic butter:**
   In a small bowl, combine melted butter, garlic, lemon juice, salt, and pepper.
3. **Grill the lobster:**
   Brush the lobster meat with the garlic butter and place it on the grill, shell side down. Grill for 6-8 minutes, basting with more butter as it cooks.
4. **Serve:**
   Serve the lobster tails with a drizzle of the garlic butter and a sprinkle of fresh parsley.

Crab Legs with Old Bay Seasoning

Ingredients:

- 2 lbs crab legs (snow or king crab)
- 1/4 cup Old Bay seasoning
- 1 tablespoon olive oil
- 2 cloves garlic, minced
- 2 tablespoons butter, melted
- Lemon wedges for serving

Instructions:

1. **Prepare the crab legs:**
   Preheat the oven to 400°F (200°C). Arrange the crab legs on a baking sheet and drizzle with olive oil and garlic.
2. **Season the crab legs:**
   Sprinkle Old Bay seasoning over the crab legs, ensuring they are evenly coated.
3. **Bake:**
   Cover the baking sheet with aluminum foil and bake for 15-20 minutes, until heated through.
4. **Serve:**
   Serve the crab legs with melted butter and lemon wedges.

Lobster Mac and Cheese

Ingredients:

- 1 lb elbow macaroni
- 1 lb lobster meat, cooked and chopped
- 2 cups shredded cheddar cheese
- 1 cup mozzarella cheese
- 1/2 cup heavy cream
- 2 cups milk
- 1/4 cup butter
- 1/4 cup flour
- 1 teaspoon mustard powder
- Salt and pepper to taste
- Fresh parsley for garnish

Instructions:

1. **Cook the pasta:**
   Cook the macaroni according to package instructions, then drain and set aside.
2. **Make the cheese sauce:**
   In a saucepan, melt butter over medium heat. Whisk in the flour and mustard powder to make a roux. Gradually add milk and heavy cream, whisking until the sauce thickens. Stir in the cheddar and mozzarella cheese until melted.
3. **Combine the lobster and pasta:**
   Stir in the lobster meat and cooked pasta into the cheese sauce. Mix well.
4. **Serve:**
   Garnish with fresh parsley and serve hot.

Crab and Corn Chowder

Ingredients:

- 1 lb crab meat, fresh or canned
- 2 cups corn kernels (fresh or frozen)
- 1 medium onion, chopped
- 2 cloves garlic, minced
- 2 cups potato, peeled and diced
- 4 cups chicken or seafood broth
- 1 cup heavy cream
- 2 tablespoons butter
- 1 teaspoon thyme
- Salt and pepper to taste
- Fresh parsley, chopped, for garnish

Instructions:

1. **Sauté the vegetables:**
   In a large pot, melt butter over medium heat. Add onions and garlic, cooking until softened, about 5 minutes.
2. **Simmer the chowder:**
   Add diced potatoes and chicken broth to the pot. Bring to a boil, then reduce heat and simmer for 10 minutes, or until potatoes are tender.
3. **Add corn and crab:**
   Stir in corn, crab meat, thyme, salt, and pepper. Let the chowder simmer for another 5-7 minutes.
4. **Add cream:**
   Pour in the heavy cream and stir to combine. Simmer for another 2-3 minutes.
5. **Serve:**
   Ladle the chowder into bowls and garnish with fresh parsley.

Lobster Thermidor

Ingredients:

- 2 lobster tails, cooked and meat removed
- 2 tablespoons butter
- 1/2 cup onion, finely chopped
- 1/4 cup white wine
- 1/4 cup heavy cream
- 1/2 cup grated Gruyère cheese
- 1 tablespoon Dijon mustard
- 1 tablespoon fresh parsley, chopped
- 1 teaspoon paprika
- Salt and pepper to taste

Instructions:

1. **Prepare the lobster:**
   Preheat the oven to 375°F (190°C). Remove the lobster meat from the tails and chop into small pieces. Set the shells aside for baking.
2. **Make the sauce:**
   In a skillet, melt butter over medium heat. Add the onions and cook until softened. Pour in the white wine and simmer for 3-4 minutes. Stir in the heavy cream, Dijon mustard, and salt and pepper to taste.
3. **Combine lobster and sauce:**
   Add the lobster meat to the sauce and cook for another 2 minutes. Remove from heat and stir in grated Gruyère cheese and fresh parsley.
4. **Stuff the lobster shells:**
   Spoon the lobster mixture back into the lobster shells and sprinkle with paprika.
5. **Bake:**
   Place the stuffed lobster tails on a baking sheet and bake for 10-12 minutes, or until the cheese is melted and bubbly.
6. **Serve:**
   Garnish with more parsley and serve hot.

Crab Imperial

Ingredients:

- 1 lb lump crab meat
- 1/4 cup mayonnaise
- 1 tablespoon Dijon mustard
- 1 tablespoon Worcestershire sauce
- 1/4 cup grated Parmesan cheese
- 1 tablespoon lemon juice
- 1/2 teaspoon Old Bay seasoning
- 1 egg, beaten
- Fresh parsley for garnish

Instructions:

1. **Preheat the oven:**
   Preheat your oven to 375°F (190°C).
2. **Prepare the crab mixture:**
   In a bowl, combine crab meat, mayonnaise, Dijon mustard, Worcestershire sauce, Parmesan cheese, lemon juice, Old Bay seasoning, and the beaten egg. Mix gently.
3. **Bake:**
   Spoon the crab mixture into a baking dish or individual ramekins. Bake for 20-25 minutes until golden on top.
4. **Serve:**
   Garnish with fresh parsley and serve hot.

Lobster and Shrimp Scampi

Ingredients:

- 2 lobster tails, cooked and chopped
- 1/2 lb shrimp, peeled and deveined
- 3 tablespoons butter
- 3 cloves garlic, minced
- 1/4 cup white wine
- 1/4 cup chicken broth
- 1/2 teaspoon red pepper flakes
- 1 tablespoon lemon juice
- 1 tablespoon fresh parsley, chopped
- Salt and pepper to taste
- Pasta (optional)

Instructions:

1. **Cook the seafood:**
   In a large skillet, melt butter over medium heat. Add garlic and red pepper flakes, sautéing for 1 minute. Add shrimp and lobster, cooking until shrimp are pink and the lobster is heated through, about 3-4 minutes.
2. **Make the sauce:**
   Add white wine, chicken broth, and lemon juice to the skillet. Bring to a simmer for 3-5 minutes.
3. **Finish the dish:**
   Stir in fresh parsley, salt, and pepper. If using pasta, toss the cooked seafood mixture with pasta.
4. **Serve:**
   Serve hot with a garnish of more parsley and lemon wedges.

Crab Dip

Ingredients:

- 1 lb crab meat, cooked and shredded
- 1/2 cup mayonnaise
- 1/2 cup sour cream
- 1 tablespoon Dijon mustard
- 1 tablespoon lemon juice
- 1 tablespoon fresh parsley, chopped
- 1 teaspoon Old Bay seasoning
- Salt and pepper to taste
- 1 cup shredded cheddar cheese

Instructions:

1. **Combine the ingredients:**
   In a bowl, mix together crab meat, mayonnaise, sour cream, Dijon mustard, lemon juice, parsley, Old Bay seasoning, salt, and pepper.
2. **Bake the dip:**
   Preheat your oven to 375°F (190°C). Transfer the mixture to a baking dish and sprinkle with shredded cheddar cheese. Bake for 15-20 minutes until the top is golden.
3. **Serve:**
   Serve warm with crackers, bread, or vegetables.

Lobster En Papillote

Ingredients:

- 2 lobster tails, split
- 2 tablespoons butter
- 1/2 cup white wine
- 1/2 teaspoon garlic powder
- 1 tablespoon lemon juice
- Fresh herbs (thyme, rosemary, parsley)
- Salt and pepper to taste
- Parchment paper

Instructions:

1. **Prepare the parchment:**
   Preheat the oven to 375°F (190°C). Cut two large sheets of parchment paper, large enough to fold over the lobster tails.
2. **Assemble the dish:**
   Place each lobster tail on a piece of parchment paper. Top with butter, white wine, garlic powder, lemon juice, fresh herbs, salt, and pepper.
3. **Seal the packets:**
   Fold the parchment paper over the lobster tails, creating a tight seal.
4. **Bake:**
   Place the packets on a baking sheet and bake for 15-20 minutes, or until the lobster is cooked through.
5. **Serve:**
   Open the parchment packets carefully and serve immediately.

Crab Claws with Lemon Butter

Ingredients:

- 1 lb crab claws
- 1/2 cup butter, melted
- 2 cloves garlic, minced
- 1 tablespoon lemon juice
- Fresh parsley, chopped, for garnish
- Lemon wedges for serving

Instructions:

1. **Prepare the crab claws:**
   Steam or boil the crab claws for 5-7 minutes until heated through.
2. **Make the lemon butter sauce:**
   In a small bowl, combine melted butter, garlic, and lemon juice.
3. **Serve:**
   Serve the crab claws with lemon butter on the side for dipping, garnished with fresh parsley and lemon wedges.

Lobster Tails with Herb Butter

Ingredients:

- 4 lobster tails, split
- 1/2 cup butter, softened
- 1 tablespoon fresh parsley, chopped
- 1 tablespoon fresh thyme, chopped
- 1 tablespoon lemon juice
- Salt and pepper to taste

Instructions:

1. **Prepare the lobster tails:**
   Preheat the oven to 375°F (190°C). Place the lobster tails on a baking sheet, split-side up.
2. **Make the herb butter:**
   In a bowl, combine softened butter, parsley, thyme, lemon juice, salt, and pepper.
3. **Apply the butter:**
   Spread the herb butter evenly over the lobster meat.
4. **Bake:**
   Bake the lobster tails for 12-15 minutes until the meat is opaque and cooked through.
5. **Serve:**
   Serve hot with extra lemon wedges.

Crab Salad

Ingredients:

- 1 lb crab meat, fresh or canned
- 1/4 cup mayonnaise
- 1 tablespoon Dijon mustard
- 1 tablespoon lemon juice
- 1 tablespoon fresh dill, chopped
- 1 tablespoon fresh parsley, chopped
- Salt and pepper to taste
- Mixed greens for serving

Instructions:

1. **Make the salad dressing:**
   In a bowl, mix mayonnaise, Dijon mustard, lemon juice, dill, parsley, salt, and pepper.
2. **Combine the crab and dressing:**
   Gently fold the crab meat into the dressing until evenly coated.
3. **Serve:**
   Serve the crab salad over a bed of mixed greens.

Lobster Poutine

Ingredients:

- 2 cups fresh lobster meat, cooked and chopped
- 2 cups French fries, cooked
- 1 cup cheese curds
- 1/2 cup lobster gravy (see instructions below)
- 1 tablespoon fresh parsley, chopped

Instructions:

1. **Make the lobster gravy:**
   In a saucepan, melt 2 tablespoons butter over medium heat. Add 1 tablespoon flour and cook for 2 minutes. Gradually whisk in 1 cup lobster stock and simmer for 5 minutes. Season with salt, pepper, and a dash of paprika.
2. **Assemble the poutine:**
   Layer the cooked fries on a plate, then top with cheese curds, lobster meat, and lobster gravy.
3. **Serve:**
   Garnish with fresh parsley and serve hot.

Crab Fritters

Ingredients:

- 1 lb crab meat, cooked and shredded
- 1 cup flour
- 1/2 cup cornmeal
- 1/2 cup milk
- 1 egg
- 1 tablespoon Dijon mustard
- 2 teaspoons Old Bay seasoning
- 1/2 teaspoon garlic powder
- Salt and pepper to taste
- Vegetable oil for frying
- Fresh parsley for garnish

Instructions:

1. **Prepare the batter:**
   In a large bowl, whisk together flour, cornmeal, Old Bay seasoning, garlic powder, salt, and pepper. In a separate bowl, beat the egg and milk together. Add to the dry ingredients and stir until combined. Fold in the crab meat.
2. **Fry the fritters:**
   Heat vegetable oil in a large skillet over medium-high heat. Drop spoonfuls of the crab batter into the hot oil, flattening slightly with the back of the spoon. Fry for 3-4 minutes on each side, or until golden brown.
3. **Drain and serve:**
   Remove from the skillet and drain on paper towels. Garnish with fresh parsley and serve hot.

Lobster Po' Boy Sandwich

Ingredients:

- 2 lobster tails, cooked and chopped
- 1/2 cup mayonnaise
- 1 tablespoon Dijon mustard
- 1 tablespoon lemon juice
- 1 teaspoon hot sauce
- Salt and pepper to taste
- 2 French rolls or po' boy bread
- Lettuce, shredded
- Tomato slices
- Pickles
- Vegetable oil for frying

Instructions:

1. **Prepare the lobster salad:**
   In a bowl, mix together mayonnaise, Dijon mustard, lemon juice, hot sauce, salt, and pepper. Fold in the chopped lobster meat.
2. **Fry the sandwich components:**
   Heat vegetable oil in a skillet. Lightly toast the rolls in the skillet, then add a few spoonfuls of lobster salad onto each roll.
3. **Assemble the sandwich:**
   Top with lettuce, tomato slices, and pickles.
4. **Serve:**
   Serve the lobster po' boy immediately, garnished with extra hot sauce if desired.

Crab Ceviche

Ingredients:

- 1 lb crab meat, fresh or canned
- 1/2 cup lime juice
- 1/4 cup lemon juice
- 1/2 cup red onion, finely chopped
- 1/2 cup cucumber, diced
- 1/2 cup tomato, diced
- 1 jalapeño, minced (optional)
- 2 tablespoons cilantro, chopped
- Salt and pepper to taste
- Tortilla chips for serving

Instructions:

1. **Prepare the ceviche:**
   In a bowl, combine crab meat, lime juice, lemon juice, onion, cucumber, tomato, and jalapeño (if using). Stir in cilantro, salt, and pepper.
2. **Marinate:**
   Let the ceviche sit in the refrigerator for at least 30 minutes to allow the flavors to meld.
3. **Serve:**
   Serve chilled with tortilla chips on the side.

Lobster Ravioli

Ingredients:

- 1 lb lobster meat, cooked and chopped
- 1 cup ricotta cheese
- 1/2 cup Parmesan cheese, grated
- 1 egg
- 1 tablespoon fresh parsley, chopped
- Salt and pepper to taste
- 1 package fresh ravioli dough or homemade dough
- 2 tablespoons butter
- 1 tablespoon olive oil
- 1 clove garlic, minced
- 1/4 cup white wine
- Fresh parsley for garnish

Instructions:

1. **Make the filling:**
   In a bowl, combine chopped lobster meat, ricotta cheese, Parmesan cheese, egg, parsley, salt, and pepper.
2. **Assemble the ravioli:**
   Roll out the ravioli dough and spoon the lobster filling onto one sheet of dough. Top with another sheet of dough and press to seal the edges. Cut into squares.
3. **Cook the ravioli:**
   Bring a pot of salted water to a boil and cook the ravioli for 3-4 minutes, or until they float to the top.
4. **Make the sauce:**
   In a skillet, melt butter and olive oil over medium heat. Add garlic and cook for 1 minute. Stir in white wine and cook for another 2-3 minutes.
5. **Serve:**
   Toss the cooked ravioli in the butter sauce, garnish with fresh parsley, and serve hot.

Crab and Avocado Salad

Ingredients:

- 1 lb crab meat, cooked and shredded
- 2 ripe avocados, diced
- 1/4 cup red onion, finely chopped
- 1 tablespoon fresh cilantro, chopped
- 1 tablespoon lime juice
- Salt and pepper to taste
- Mixed greens for serving

Instructions:

1. **Prepare the salad:**
   In a bowl, gently mix crab meat, diced avocados, red onion, cilantro, lime juice, salt, and pepper.
2. **Serve:**
   Serve the salad over a bed of mixed greens and enjoy immediately.

Lobster and Crab Stuffed Lobster

Ingredients:

- 2 lobster tails, split
- 1/2 lb crab meat, cooked
- 1/2 lb lobster meat, cooked and chopped
- 1/2 cup breadcrumbs
- 1/4 cup Parmesan cheese, grated
- 1/4 cup fresh parsley, chopped
- 1 egg
- 2 tablespoons butter, melted
- 1 tablespoon lemon juice
- Salt and pepper to taste

Instructions:

1. **Prepare the stuffing:**
   In a bowl, combine crab meat, lobster meat, breadcrumbs, Parmesan cheese, parsley, egg, melted butter, lemon juice, salt, and pepper.
2. **Stuff the lobster:**
   Spoon the stuffing mixture into the lobster shells, pressing down gently to pack the filling.
3. **Bake:**
   Preheat the oven to 375°F (190°C). Place the stuffed lobster tails on a baking sheet and bake for 15-20 minutes, or until the stuffing is golden and the lobster is cooked through.
4. **Serve:**
   Serve hot with lemon wedges.

Crab Louie Salad

Ingredients:

- 1 lb crab meat, cooked and shredded
- 4 cups mixed lettuce
- 2 hard-boiled eggs, sliced
- 1 tomato, sliced
- 1/4 cup sliced cucumber
- 1/4 cup green onions, chopped
- 1/2 cup Louie dressing (see instructions below)

Louie Dressing:

- 1/2 cup mayonnaise
- 2 tablespoons ketchup
- 1 tablespoon Dijon mustard
- 1 teaspoon lemon juice
- 1 teaspoon hot sauce (optional)
- Salt and pepper to taste

Instructions:

1. **Make the dressing:**
   In a bowl, whisk together mayonnaise, ketchup, Dijon mustard, lemon juice, hot sauce, salt, and pepper.
2. **Assemble the salad:**
   Arrange lettuce, tomato, cucumber, green onions, and hard-boiled eggs on plates. Top with crab meat.
3. **Serve:**
   Drizzle with Louie dressing and serve immediately.

Lobster Pappardelle

Ingredients:

- 2 lobster tails, cooked and chopped
- 1 lb pappardelle pasta
- 2 tablespoons olive oil
- 2 cloves garlic, minced
- 1/2 cup white wine
- 1/2 cup heavy cream
- 1/2 cup Parmesan cheese, grated
- Fresh parsley for garnish
- Salt and pepper to taste

Instructions:

1. **Cook the pasta:**
   Cook pappardelle pasta according to package instructions. Drain and set aside.
2. **Make the sauce:**
   In a large skillet, heat olive oil over medium heat. Add garlic and cook for 1 minute. Add white wine and cook for 3-4 minutes. Stir in heavy cream and Parmesan cheese, and simmer for 2-3 minutes.
3. **Combine:**
   Add the lobster meat to the sauce and cook for an additional 2 minutes. Toss in the cooked pasta and stir to coat.
4. **Serve:**
   Garnish with fresh parsley and serve hot.

Crabmeat Omelette

Ingredients:

- 1/2 lb crab meat, cooked and shredded
- 4 eggs
- 2 tablespoons butter
- 1/4 cup heavy cream
- 1 tablespoon fresh chives, chopped
- Salt and pepper to taste

Instructions:

1. **Prepare the omelette:**
   In a bowl, whisk eggs, heavy cream, salt, and pepper. Heat butter in a skillet over medium heat.
2. **Cook the omelette:**
   Pour the egg mixture into the skillet and cook for 2-3 minutes until the edges begin to set. Add the crab meat and chives to the center, then fold the omelette in half.
3. **Serve:**
   Serve immediately, garnished with extra chives if desired.

Lobster and Crab Linguine

Ingredients:

- 1/2 lb lobster meat, cooked and chopped
- 1/2 lb crab meat, cooked and shredded
- 1 lb linguine pasta
- 2 tablespoons olive oil
- 3 cloves garlic, minced
- 1/2 cup white wine
- 1/2 cup heavy cream
- 1 tablespoon fresh parsley, chopped
- Salt and pepper to taste

Instructions:

1. **Cook the pasta:**
   Cook linguine pasta according to package instructions. Drain and set aside.
2. **Make the sauce:**
   In a large skillet, heat olive oil over medium heat. Add garlic and cook for 1 minute. Add white wine and simmer for 3-4 minutes. Stir in heavy cream and simmer for 2-3 minutes.
3. **Combine:**
   Add lobster and crab meat to the skillet and cook for 2-3 minutes. Toss in the cooked pasta and stir to combine.
4. **Serve:**
   Garnish with fresh parsley and serve immediately.

Crab Boil

Ingredients:

- 2 lbs crab legs
- 4 ears corn, cut into halves
- 1 lb baby potatoes, halved
- 2 tablespoons Old Bay seasoning
- 1 tablespoon garlic powder
- 1 lemon, halved
- 4 cloves garlic, smashed
- 4-6 cups water
- 1/4 cup butter, melted
- Fresh parsley for garnish

Instructions:

1. **Prepare the water:**
   In a large pot, fill with water to cover the ingredients. Add Old Bay seasoning, garlic powder, garlic cloves, and lemon halves. Bring to a boil.
2. **Boil the ingredients:**
   Add the baby potatoes and corn to the pot. Cook for 10 minutes, then add the crab legs and cook for an additional 5-7 minutes, or until the crab legs are fully heated through.
3. **Serve:**
   Drain the boil and transfer everything to a large serving tray. Drizzle with melted butter and garnish with fresh parsley.

Lobster Tacos

Ingredients:

- 2 lobster tails, cooked and chopped
- 8 small soft tortillas
- 1/2 cup shredded lettuce
- 1/2 cup diced tomatoes
- 1/4 cup red onion, thinly sliced
- 1/4 cup fresh cilantro, chopped
- 1/4 cup sour cream
- 1 tablespoon lime juice
- 1 teaspoon chili powder
- Salt and pepper to taste

Instructions:

1. **Prepare the lobster filling:**
   In a bowl, mix the lobster meat with chili powder, lime juice, salt, and pepper.
2. **Assemble the tacos:**
   Warm the tortillas in a skillet or microwave. Spread a spoonful of sour cream on each tortilla, then top with lobster, shredded lettuce, tomatoes, onions, and cilantro.
3. **Serve:**
   Serve immediately with extra lime wedges on the side.

Crab and Spinach Stuffed Artichokes

Ingredients:

- 4 large artichokes
- 1/2 lb crab meat, cooked and shredded
- 1 cup fresh spinach, chopped
- 1/2 cup breadcrumbs
- 1/4 cup grated Parmesan cheese
- 1/4 cup mayonnaise
- 1 teaspoon garlic powder
- Salt and pepper to taste
- 2 tablespoons butter, melted

Instructions:

1. **Prepare the artichokes:**
   Trim the artichokes, removing the tough outer leaves, and cut off the tops. Steam the artichokes for 25-30 minutes, or until tender.
2. **Make the stuffing:**
   In a bowl, combine crab meat, spinach, breadcrumbs, Parmesan cheese, mayonnaise, garlic powder, salt, and pepper.
3. **Stuff the artichokes:**
   Carefully pull the leaves of the artichokes apart and spoon the crab mixture into the centers.
4. **Bake:**
   Preheat the oven to 375°F (190°C). Place the stuffed artichokes on a baking sheet and drizzle with melted butter. Bake for 15-20 minutes, or until the stuffing is golden brown.
5. **Serve:**
   Serve hot with a drizzle of extra butter if desired.

Lobster Bisque Gratin

Ingredients:

- 1 lb lobster meat, cooked and chopped
- 2 cups lobster bisque (store-bought or homemade)
- 1/2 cup heavy cream
- 1 tablespoon brandy (optional)
- 1/2 cup breadcrumbs
- 1/4 cup grated Gruyère cheese
- Fresh parsley for garnish

Instructions:

1. **Prepare the bisque base:**
   In a pot, heat lobster bisque and heavy cream over medium heat. Add the brandy if using, and stir in the lobster meat. Cook until heated through.
2. **Make the gratin topping:**
   In a small bowl, mix breadcrumbs and grated Gruyère cheese.
3. **Assemble and bake:**
   Pour the lobster bisque mixture into small oven-safe bowls. Sprinkle the breadcrumb and cheese mixture on top. Preheat the broiler and place the bowls under the broiler for 3-5 minutes, or until the topping is golden and crispy.
4. **Serve:**
   Garnish with fresh parsley and serve immediately.

Crab Wellington

Ingredients:

- 1 lb crab meat, cooked and shredded
- 1 sheet puff pastry, thawed
- 1/4 cup cream cheese, softened
- 1/4 cup Dijon mustard
- 1 tablespoon fresh dill, chopped
- 1 egg, beaten
- 1 tablespoon olive oil
- Salt and pepper to taste

Instructions:

1. **Prepare the filling:**
   In a bowl, combine crab meat, cream cheese, Dijon mustard, dill, salt, and pepper.
2. **Assemble the Wellington:**
   Roll out the puff pastry on a floured surface. Spread the crab mixture in the center, then fold the pastry over to encase the crab. Seal the edges and brush with the beaten egg.
3. **Bake:**
   Preheat the oven to 375°F (190°C). Place the Wellington on a baking sheet and bake for 25-30 minutes, or until golden brown and puffed.
4. **Serve:**
   Slice and serve immediately.

Lobster with Mango Salsa

Ingredients:

- 2 lobster tails, cooked and split
- 1 mango, peeled and diced
- 1/4 cup red onion, finely chopped
- 1 tablespoon lime juice
- 1 tablespoon fresh cilantro, chopped
- 1 tablespoon olive oil
- Salt and pepper to taste

Instructions:

1. **Prepare the salsa:**
   In a bowl, combine mango, red onion, lime juice, cilantro, olive oil, salt, and pepper. Toss gently.
2. **Serve:**
   Spoon the mango salsa over the split lobster tails and serve immediately.

Crab Mac and Cheese

Ingredients:

- 1/2 lb crab meat, cooked and shredded
- 8 oz elbow macaroni
- 2 tablespoons butter
- 2 tablespoons flour
- 2 cups milk
- 2 cups shredded cheddar cheese
- 1/2 cup grated Parmesan cheese
- Salt and pepper to taste
- 1/2 teaspoon garlic powder
- 1/4 cup breadcrumbs (optional)

Instructions:

1. **Cook the pasta:**
   Cook the elbow macaroni according to package instructions. Drain and set aside.
2. **Make the cheese sauce:**
   In a large saucepan, melt butter over medium heat. Stir in the flour and cook for 1 minute. Gradually add milk, whisking to prevent lumps. Stir in cheddar cheese, Parmesan, garlic powder, salt, and pepper. Continue cooking until the sauce thickens.
3. **Combine the pasta and crab:**
   Stir the cooked macaroni and crab meat into the cheese sauce.
4. **Bake (optional):**
   If desired, transfer the mixture to a baking dish, sprinkle breadcrumbs on top, and bake at 375°F (190°C) for 15-20 minutes, or until golden and bubbly.
5. **Serve:**
   Serve hot.

Lobster and Corn Fritters

Ingredients:

- 1 lb lobster meat, cooked and chopped
- 1 cup corn kernels (fresh or frozen)
- 1/2 cup flour
- 1/2 teaspoon baking powder
- 1/4 teaspoon paprika
- 1/4 teaspoon salt
- 1 egg, beaten
- 1/2 cup milk
- Vegetable oil for frying

Instructions:

1. **Prepare the batter:**
   In a bowl, combine flour, baking powder, paprika, salt, egg, and milk. Fold in the lobster meat and corn.
2. **Fry the fritters:**
   Heat vegetable oil in a large skillet over medium-high heat. Drop spoonfuls of the batter into the hot oil and fry for 3-4 minutes on each side, or until golden brown.
3. **Serve:**
   Drain on paper towels and serve hot.

Crab Alfredo

Ingredients:

- 1/2 lb crab meat, cooked and shredded
- 1 lb fettuccine pasta
- 2 tablespoons butter
- 2 cloves garlic, minced
- 1 cup heavy cream
- 1 cup grated Parmesan cheese
- Salt and pepper to taste
- Fresh parsley for garnish

Instructions:

1. **Cook the pasta:**
   Cook fettuccine pasta according to package instructions. Drain and set aside.
2. **Make the Alfredo sauce:**
   In a large skillet, melt butter over medium heat. Add garlic and cook for 1 minute. Stir in heavy cream and cook for 2-3 minutes. Add Parmesan cheese and stir until melted.
3. **Combine the pasta and crab:**
   Add the crab meat to the Alfredo sauce and stir to combine. Toss in the cooked pasta and mix well.
4. **Serve:**
   Garnish with fresh parsley and serve hot.

Lobster Salad with Lemon Vinaigrette

Ingredients:

- 2 lobster tails, cooked and chopped
- 4 cups mixed greens (arugula, spinach, and romaine)
- 1/2 cucumber, thinly sliced
- 1/2 red onion, thinly sliced
- 1/4 cup cherry tomatoes, halved
- 2 tablespoons olive oil
- 1 tablespoon lemon juice
- 1 teaspoon Dijon mustard
- Salt and pepper to taste
- 1 tablespoon fresh parsley, chopped

Instructions:

1. **Prepare the salad:**
   In a large bowl, toss together the mixed greens, cucumber, red onion, and cherry tomatoes.
2. **Make the vinaigrette:**
   In a small bowl, whisk together olive oil, lemon juice, Dijon mustard, salt, and pepper.
3. **Assemble the salad:**
   Top the salad with chopped lobster meat. Drizzle with the lemon vinaigrette and garnish with fresh parsley.
4. **Serve:**
   Serve immediately for a refreshing, light meal.

Crab-Stuffed Bell Peppers

Ingredients:

- 2 large bell peppers, halved and seeded
- 1 lb crab meat, cooked and shredded
- 1/2 cup cooked rice
- 1/4 cup breadcrumbs
- 1/4 cup grated Parmesan cheese
- 2 tablespoons mayonnaise
- 1 teaspoon Old Bay seasoning
- 1 tablespoon fresh parsley, chopped
- 1 tablespoon lemon juice
- Salt and pepper to taste
- 2 tablespoons olive oil

Instructions:

1. **Prepare the peppers:**
   Preheat the oven to 375°F (190°C). Place the halved bell peppers in a baking dish and drizzle with olive oil. Bake for 10-15 minutes, until slightly tender.
2. **Make the stuffing:**
   In a bowl, combine crab meat, cooked rice, breadcrumbs, Parmesan cheese, mayonnaise, Old Bay seasoning, parsley, lemon juice, salt, and pepper.
3. **Stuff the peppers:**
   Spoon the crab mixture into the baked bell pepper halves.
4. **Bake the stuffed peppers:**
   Return the stuffed peppers to the oven and bake for another 15-20 minutes, until the filling is golden and heated through.
5. **Serve:**
   Serve hot with a sprinkle of fresh parsley on top.

Lobster Sautéed with Garlic and Wine

Ingredients:

- 2 lobster tails, shelled and cut into pieces
- 2 tablespoons butter
- 2 cloves garlic, minced
- 1/2 cup white wine
- 1 tablespoon fresh lemon juice
- 1 tablespoon fresh parsley, chopped
- Salt and pepper to taste

Instructions:

1. **Sauté the lobster:**
   In a large skillet, melt butter over medium heat. Add the garlic and cook for 1 minute, until fragrant. Add the lobster pieces and sauté for 3-4 minutes, until the lobster is just cooked.
2. **Deglaze the pan:**
   Pour in the white wine and lemon juice, scraping up any bits from the bottom of the pan. Cook for another 2-3 minutes, allowing the sauce to reduce slightly.
3. **Serve:**
   Season with salt and pepper, and sprinkle with fresh parsley. Serve immediately with crusty bread or over pasta.

Crab Croquettes

Ingredients:

- 1 lb crab meat, cooked and shredded
- 1/2 cup breadcrumbs, plus more for coating
- 1/4 cup grated Parmesan cheese
- 2 tablespoons mayonnaise
- 1 tablespoon Dijon mustard
- 1 egg, beaten
- 1 tablespoon fresh parsley, chopped
- 1 tablespoon lemon juice
- Salt and pepper to taste
- Vegetable oil for frying

Instructions:

1. **Make the croquette mixture:**
   In a bowl, combine crab meat, breadcrumbs, Parmesan cheese, mayonnaise, Dijon mustard, egg, parsley, lemon juice, salt, and pepper.
2. **Form the croquettes:**
   Shape the mixture into small patties or balls and coat each one in additional breadcrumbs.
3. **Fry the croquettes:**
   Heat vegetable oil in a skillet over medium heat. Fry the croquettes in batches for 3-4 minutes on each side, or until golden brown.
4. **Serve:**
   Drain on paper towels and serve with a side of lemon wedges and a dipping sauce of your choice.

Lobster Tail with Lemon Aioli

Ingredients:

- 2 lobster tails, cut down the center
- 1 tablespoon olive oil
- 1 teaspoon smoked paprika
- Salt and pepper to taste
- 1/4 cup mayonnaise
- 1 tablespoon fresh lemon juice
- 1 garlic clove, minced
- 1 tablespoon fresh parsley, chopped

Instructions:

1. **Prepare the lobster:**
   Preheat the grill to medium-high heat. Brush the lobster tails with olive oil and season with smoked paprika, salt, and pepper.
2. **Grill the lobster:**
   Grill the lobster tails, shell side down, for about 5-7 minutes, until the meat is opaque and fully cooked.
3. **Make the aioli:**
   In a small bowl, combine mayonnaise, lemon juice, garlic, and parsley. Stir until smooth.
4. **Serve:**
   Serve the lobster tails with a generous drizzle of lemon aioli on top.

Crab-Stuffed Mushrooms

Ingredients:

- 12 large button mushrooms, stems removed
- 1/2 lb crab meat, cooked and shredded
- 1/4 cup breadcrumbs
- 2 tablespoons cream cheese, softened
- 2 tablespoons grated Parmesan cheese
- 1 teaspoon garlic powder
- 1 tablespoon fresh parsley, chopped
- 1 tablespoon lemon juice
- Salt and pepper to taste
- Olive oil for drizzling

Instructions:

1. **Prepare the mushrooms:**
   Preheat the oven to 375°F (190°C). Arrange the mushroom caps on a baking sheet and drizzle with olive oil.
2. **Make the stuffing:**
   In a bowl, combine crab meat, breadcrumbs, cream cheese, Parmesan cheese, garlic powder, parsley, lemon juice, salt, and pepper.
3. **Stuff the mushrooms:**
   Spoon the crab mixture into the mushroom caps.
4. **Bake the stuffed mushrooms:**
   Bake for 15-20 minutes, until the mushrooms are tender and the filling is golden.
5. **Serve:**
   Serve hot as an appetizer or part of a seafood meal.

Lobster and Crab Risotto

Ingredients:

- 1/2 lb lobster meat, cooked and chopped
- 1/2 lb crab meat, cooked and shredded
- 1 1/2 cups Arborio rice
- 4 cups seafood stock (or chicken stock)
- 1/2 cup dry white wine
- 1 small onion, finely chopped
- 2 cloves garlic, minced
- 2 tablespoons butter
- 1/2 cup Parmesan cheese, grated
- 1/4 cup heavy cream
- Salt and pepper to taste
- Fresh parsley, chopped for garnish

Instructions:

1. **Prepare the stock:**
   In a saucepan, heat the seafood stock and keep it warm over low heat.
2. **Cook the rice:**
   In a large skillet or pot, melt butter over medium heat. Add the chopped onion and garlic and sauté for 2-3 minutes until softened. Add the Arborio rice and cook for 1-2 minutes, stirring to coat the rice with butter.
3. **Add the wine:**
   Pour in the white wine and stir until it is mostly absorbed.
4. **Cook the risotto:**
   Gradually add the warm stock to the rice, one ladle at a time, stirring constantly. Wait until the liquid is absorbed before adding more stock. Continue this process for 18-20 minutes, until the rice is tender and creamy.
5. **Finish the risotto:**
   Stir in the lobster and crab meat, Parmesan cheese, and heavy cream. Season with salt and pepper to taste.
6. **Serve:**
   Garnish with fresh parsley and serve hot.

Crab and Lobster Bisque Soup

Ingredients:

- 1/2 lb lobster meat, cooked and chopped
- 1/2 lb crab meat, cooked and shredded
- 4 cups seafood stock
- 1/2 cup heavy cream
- 1/4 cup dry white wine
- 1 small onion, chopped
- 2 cloves garlic, minced
- 1 carrot, chopped
- 1 celery stalk, chopped
- 2 tablespoons butter
- 1 tablespoon tomato paste
- 1/2 teaspoon paprika
- Salt and pepper to taste
- Fresh parsley, for garnish

Instructions:

1. **Sauté the vegetables:**
   In a large pot, melt butter over medium heat. Add the onion, garlic, carrot, and celery. Cook for 5-7 minutes, stirring occasionally, until softened.
2. **Add the tomato paste and spices:**
   Stir in the tomato paste and paprika, cooking for another 2 minutes.
3. **Add the stock and wine:**
   Pour in the seafood stock and white wine. Bring to a boil, then reduce to a simmer for 15-20 minutes.
4. **Puree the soup:**
   Use an immersion blender or transfer the soup to a blender and puree until smooth.
5. **Add cream and seafood:**
   Return the soup to the pot and stir in the heavy cream, lobster, and crab meat. Season with salt and pepper. Heat through for 5 minutes.
6. **Serve:**
   Ladle the bisque into bowls, garnish with fresh parsley, and serve hot.

Lobster and Crab Ramen

Ingredients:

- 1/2 lb lobster meat, cooked and chopped
- 1/2 lb crab meat, cooked and shredded
- 2 packs ramen noodles (discard seasoning packet)
- 4 cups seafood stock
- 2 tablespoons soy sauce
- 1 tablespoon sesame oil
- 1 teaspoon ginger, grated
- 2 cloves garlic, minced
- 1 tablespoon miso paste (optional)
- 2 eggs, soft-boiled
- 1 green onion, chopped
- Fresh cilantro for garnish
- Lime wedges

Instructions:

1. **Prepare the broth:**
   In a pot, combine the seafood stock, soy sauce, sesame oil, ginger, garlic, and miso paste (if using). Bring to a simmer for 5-7 minutes.
2. **Cook the noodles:**
   In another pot, cook the ramen noodles according to package instructions. Drain and set aside.
3. **Assemble the ramen:**
   Divide the cooked noodles between two bowls. Pour the hot broth over the noodles.
4. **Add the seafood and eggs:**
   Top with lobster and crab meat, a soft-boiled egg, green onions, and cilantro. Serve with lime wedges on the side.
5. **Serve:**
   Serve immediately and enjoy your luxurious seafood ramen!

Crab and Lobster Gratin

Ingredients:

- 1/2 lb lobster meat, cooked and chopped
- 1/2 lb crab meat, cooked and shredded
- 1 cup heavy cream
- 1/2 cup Parmesan cheese, grated
- 1/4 cup breadcrumbs
- 2 tablespoons butter
- 1 tablespoon all-purpose flour
- 1/2 cup dry white wine
- 1/4 teaspoon nutmeg
- Salt and pepper to taste
- Fresh parsley for garnish

Instructions:

1. **Prepare the sauce:**
   Preheat the oven to 375°F (190°C). In a saucepan, melt butter over medium heat. Stir in the flour and cook for 1 minute. Gradually whisk in the white wine and heavy cream, and cook until the sauce thickens (about 5 minutes). Add the nutmeg, salt, and pepper.
2. **Add the seafood:**
   Stir in the lobster and crab meat, then pour the mixture into a greased baking dish.
3. **Top with breadcrumbs:**
   Sprinkle the Parmesan cheese and breadcrumbs over the seafood mixture.
4. **Bake:**
   Bake for 15-20 minutes, or until the top is golden brown.
5. **Serve:**
   Garnish with fresh parsley and serve hot.

Lobster and Crab Cakes with Remoulade

Ingredients:

- 1/2 lb lobster meat, cooked and chopped
- 1/2 lb crab meat, cooked and shredded
- 1/2 cup breadcrumbs
- 2 tablespoons mayonnaise
- 1 tablespoon Dijon mustard
- 1 egg, beaten
- 2 tablespoons fresh parsley, chopped
- 1 tablespoon lemon juice
- 1 teaspoon Old Bay seasoning
- Salt and pepper to taste
- 1 tablespoon olive oil for frying

For the remoulade sauce:

- 1/2 cup mayonnaise
- 1 tablespoon Dijon mustard
- 1 tablespoon ketchup
- 1 tablespoon lemon juice
- 1 teaspoon hot sauce
- 1 tablespoon capers, chopped
- 1 tablespoon fresh parsley, chopped

Instructions:

1. **Make the cakes:**
   In a large bowl, combine lobster, crab, breadcrumbs, mayonnaise, Dijon mustard, egg, parsley, lemon juice, Old Bay seasoning, salt, and pepper. Form into small patties.
2. **Cook the cakes:**
   Heat olive oil in a skillet over medium heat. Cook the crab and lobster cakes for 3-4 minutes per side, until golden and crispy.
3. **Make the remoulade sauce:**
   In a small bowl, mix together the mayonnaise, Dijon mustard, ketchup, lemon juice, hot sauce, capers, and parsley.
4. **Serve:**
   Serve the crab and lobster cakes with the remoulade sauce on the side.

Crab and Lobster Bruschetta

Ingredients:

- 1/2 lb lobster meat, cooked and chopped
- 1/2 lb crab meat, cooked and shredded
- 1 baguette, sliced into 1-inch pieces
- 2 tablespoons olive oil
- 2 cloves garlic, minced
- 1/2 cup fresh basil, chopped
- 1/4 cup Parmesan cheese, grated
- 1 tablespoon lemon juice
- Salt and pepper to taste

Instructions:

1. **Toast the bread:**
   Preheat the oven to 375°F (190°C). Place the baguette slices on a baking sheet and brush with olive oil. Toast in the oven for 5-7 minutes, until golden brown.
2. **Prepare the topping:**
   In a bowl, combine lobster, crab, garlic, basil, Parmesan cheese, lemon juice, salt, and pepper.
3. **Assemble the bruschetta:**
   Spoon the seafood mixture onto the toasted bread slices.
4. **Serve:**
   Serve immediately as an appetizer or snack.

www.ingramcontent.com/pod-product-compliance
Lightning Source LLC
LaVergne TN
LVHW081340060526
838201LV00055B/2774